GreenSpirit
REFLECTIONS

GreenSpirit book series

GREENSPIRIT
REFLECTIONS

Compiled by Santoshan (Stephen Wollaston)

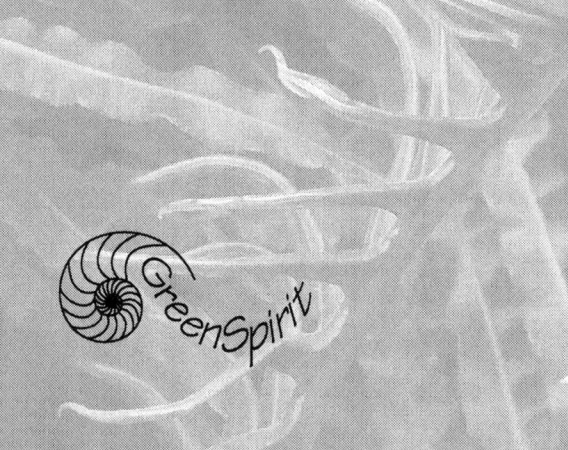

Independent Publishing Platform
Distributed and printed by Amazon

Title No. 10 in the GreenSpirit Book Series
www.greenspirit.org.uk
GreenSpirit is a registered charity based in the UK. The main contents/written material, editing, design and promotional work for its books is done on a purely voluntary basis or given freely by contributors who share a passion for Gaia-centred spirituality.

© Santoshan (Stephen Wollaston) 2020

First edition
ISBN 9798633141962
A low-cost eBook edition of *GreenSpirit Reflections* is also available.

All rights reserved. Except for brief quotations in critical articles or reviews, no part of this book may be reproduced in any manner without prior written permission from the compiler.

Design and artwork by Santoshan (Stephen Wollaston)
Cover photo Nerthus/Pixabay.com

Copyright Images:
Page 7 photo © My Good Images/Shutterstock.com
Page 12 photo © Natalia Deriabina/Shutterstock.com
Page 21 photo © Danm12/Shutterstock.com
Page 32 illustration © Argus/Shutterstock.com
Page 75 vector © Dedoma/Shutterstock.com
Page 76 photo © inLite studio/Shutterstock.com
Page 93 photo © Pasko Maksim/Shutterstock.com
Page 113-114 photo © KMN Photo/Shutterstock.com

Contents

Introduction 7
1 Awakening 11
2 GreenSpirit 21
3 Earth 31
4 Nature 39
5 Interconnectedness 53
6 Evolvement 65
7 Stories 75
8 The Numinous 85
9 Engagement 93
References 107
GreenSpirit Resources 113

To lovers of the Earth.

Introduction

reenSpirit Reflections is the tenth title in the GreenSpirit Book Series, which is a low-cost series on Earth-centred spirituality, sold at production price only. This book brings together a collection of key passages from various GreenSpirit titles. Apart from quotations by Thomas Berry, which are from another GreenSpirit anthology (*Meditations with Thomas Berry*), all other passages are by contributors and editors of numerous articles and authors of titles published by GreenSpirit in a total of eleven books. Some writers' names appear more than others because they have written a complete book for GreenSpirit or are the contributors and editors of several titles, which meant there was more material by them to draw upon and include in the following pages. The References section at the back lists page numbers and titles from where each quotation was taken.

Having worked on the design of two previous meditations books, and editing one of them, I guess I can lay claim to possessing a knack for putting books of this kind together. Like many titles, the initial idea of compiling it, organically grew from what had been done before. Yet the idea of a collection of quotations for reflection and meditation purposes, turned into something greater than first expected. On completion, a fellow GreenSpirit colleague commented how it clearly flowed easily from one section to another like a short-course on green spirituality. With this in mind, the advice usually given to readers for anthologies of quotations about *starting at any place*, needs to be accompanied by an extra recommendation of also reflecting and meditating on the passages by *starting with the first one and gradually reading through to the last*. Passages can of course be used in various ways, such as reading them aloud for ceremonial and ritual purposes.

Suggestions for How to Use this Book
If you require some guidance about how to use this book, you may find the following suggestions helpful.

First, find a peaceful place on your own or with a small group of friends in your home or garden, or in the countryside or a tranquil special place of worship. Take time to be still and quieten your mind. Sit in an upright position, with the spine erect. Feel the weight of your body on the chair, cushion or ground you are sitting on. Be aware of your interconnectedness with Gaia, with Mother Earth, with how the plants and trees feed you with life-giving oxygen and in return your breath feeds them. Consciously release any tension in your mind and body by taking a gentle deep breath and feeling it gently flowing into your lungs, noticing your upper-chest and abdomen rising naturally, and when you breathe out, slowly and gently exhale and release any tension with the out-breath. Set the intension of seeking to be one with the natural world and in harmony with all

INTRODUCTION

that is within and around you. Notice any sounds of Nature such as bird song, rustling leaves or noises made by animal friends as they go about their daily lives.

Now allow your breathing to find its own natural rhythm. Select one of the passages you feel drawn to in this book, or open it randomly on a page or start at the beginning. Read the passage slowly. If you are with friends, select one amongst you to read the passage aloud. Reflect upon what the words mean to you. Be with your reflective thoughts and feelings for a while and see what arises with a sense of open-hearted receptiveness. Take your time doing this. You may feel the need to read the passage again and to repeat some of the above steps. You may also wish to reflect upon other passages in the book during this time.

If you are doing this with friends, you will probably want to share any reflective thoughts or feelings that come to you. If on your own, you may wish to write them down in a spiritual journal and come back to what you write for further reflection another time. Your reflections may reveal an action you feel deeply impelled to act upon. By writing down your thoughts and feelings, what might be a fleeting moment of insight and inspiration, will not be forgotten, and may even lead you to new ways of being and relating to Earth-life and its abundant beauty.

All of the above can be done as an exercise in itself, as a preliminary step for another type of practice or part of a day of various contemplative exercises and rituals. Traditionally, in contemplative Christian spirituality, a short passage of scripture is often reflected upon for the purpose of awakening to mystical union with the divine, which is popularly known as *Lectio Divina*, divine reading, in the Christian tradition. But the practice of reflecting upon a text to achieve new levels of insight is found in many traditions, including nonreligious ones.

I trust that the following pages will supply you with some nourishment on your spiritual journey, and will awaken you to embracing the profound unity we all share with the more-than-human queendoms and kingdoms of the natural world.

~ Santoshan (Stephen Wollaston)

* * *

Awakening

1

AWAKENING

It is clear that humanity has lost its way and that only a profound personal and collective transformation can bring about the change we need.

~ Joyce Edmond-Smith

We have been so successful as a species that our success has gone to our heads. Over the generations we have developed a lifestyle that is based on wealth and power, and this has alienated us from the natural world on which we depend for our survival.

~ Joan Angus

AWAKENING

We have been like sleepwalkers,
moving with closed eyes towards a precipice.
But at last,
and maybe only just in time,
we are beginning to wake up.

~ Marian Van Eyk McCain

Once we truly understand that we are the Earth, that the Earth is a living, conscious being and that it is NOT all about us; we shall surely recognise that our health and Gaia's health are not just connected but utterly intertwined, joined and interdependent. They are one and the same. Our healing and the wellbeing of all life are dependent on Gaia's healing. Neither we nor any other living organism can be healthy unless Gaia is healthy.

~ Sky McCain

AWAKENING

If we are to continue living with Mother Earth,
we need to not only care about the diversity of life she has
sought to celebrate but also learn how to read her signs,
understand her ways and adapt creatively to living in
harmony with her.

~ Santoshan (Stephen Wollaston)

When you awaken awe, you awaken reverence
and you awaken gratitude.
~ Matthew Fox

AWAKENING

We can honour nonhuman nature, nurturing it within the concrete jungles of our planet, but each day we must also learn how to better inspire our fellow humans, making sure that what we add to the currents of human nature is positive.

~ Emma Restall Orr

If we take a leaf from the pages of Nature, which are about diversity and equilibrium, we can learn how to go forward. If we follow her example and are maturely sensitive enough to the differences that make up our human race, and appreciate how human life is enriched by its different people, beliefs and cultures, we can start to find ways of living peacefully with one another and working together for the betterment of all.

~ Santoshan (Stephen Wollaston)

GreenSpirit

2

To live in the world from a GreenSpirit orientation is to see oneself as being *of* the Earth rather than *on* it and to see the planetary ecosystem as a whole (rather than humans) as being of central importance in everything and at all times.

~ Marian Van Eyk McCain

Thankfully, Nature centred spiritualities have never been completely forgotten and are these days starting to become centre stage once again, as now, more than ever, there is a growing paramount need to revive and strengthen our kinship with Earth and to act justly, responsibly and wisely for our times.

~ Santoshan (Stephen Wollaston)

The journey this inner reconnection takes us on is not for the fainthearted. It is the ancient journey to enlightenment, once the province of saints and mystics but now perhaps a condition of our continued existence on Planet Earth. We do not need only a new understanding but more profoundly we need a new way of being.

~ June Raymond

The radical vision of GreenSpirit brings together the rigor
of science, the creativity of artistic expression,
the passion of social action and the core wisdom that
exists within the spiritual traditions of all ages.
~ A popular summary about GreenSpirit

If there is to be real and sustainable progress,
it must be a continuing enhancement of life for the entire
planetary community. It must be shared by all the living,
from the plankton in the sea to the birds above the land.
It must include the grasses, the trees,
and the living creatures of the earth.

~ Thomas Berry

So far, what I most love about this way of life is having more time, flexibility and autonomy for the things that really matter to me. For me this has been as much a spiritual journey and awakening as anything else.

~ Sally Lever

For me, GreenSpirit is about love and gratitude.
Seeing the world as blessing, learning to love it and
seeking to share it with others.
The longer I live, the more I realise
how privileged I am to be here.
~ Brendan Caulfield-James

A GreenSpirit way of seeing the world is not based purely on the pragmatic need to develop a sustainable way of life for humans in order to prevent ecological collapse. It also grew out of the hunger for meaning, for a deep sense of connectedness and for a spiritual dimension to *everything* we do and feel and experience ~ the way we live, eat, work, play, celebrate and carry out all the functions of our day.
~ Marian Van Eyk McCain

Earth

3

EARTH

The Ancient Greeks understood the Earth as a mother and called her Gaia.
It has now been scientifically recognized and acknowledged that Gaia acts as an intelligent, evolving, sustainable, self-regulatory and living being.

~ Ruth Meyers

A Gaian approach opens new doors of perception and opens up our vision of the interdependence of all things within the natural world.

~ Stephan Harding

EARTH

To understand Gaia, to let her into our lives, we must fall in love with the Earth. It's that simple.

~ Susan Meeker-Lowry

What if we fully acknowledged our total dependence on Gaia and her elements and came to the realization that Nature is not only around us but also within us and that we are cells in the body of a living planet?

~ Marian Van Eyk McCain

EARTH

When our love of the Earth and our astonishment,
our marvelling, our wonder and reverence for the vastness
and mystery of the universe becomes the focus of our
spiritual lives, rather than some far off, dreamed-of heaven,
then just as the Earth feeds our bodies,
she also feeds our souls.

~ Marian Van Eyk McCain

Earth is not a static backdrop for the evolution of plants and animals; rather the atmosphere, rocks and biosphere together enact an exquisitely intricate dance of holistic evolution.

~ Greg Morter

Nature

4

NATURE

Nature is full of wonder and surprises.

~ Nigel Lees

Nature does not belong to humans,

humans belong to Nature,

humans are Nature,

there is no distinction.

~ Satish Kumar

NATURE

Nature is something we are; not just something with which we relate. In the beauty of following Nature as a spiritual path comes an ability to recognize that: to feel Nature's order in ourselves as well as in every surrounding.

~ Eric Alan

I walk in Nature, not as an escape from the strain and stress of urban life, not for entertainment or sightseeing, not even as a scientist looking at Nature as an object of study. I go in Nature as a pilgrim for the renewal of my spirit. Walking in Nature is my meditation and my prayer. The magnificent trees and majestic hills are my temples and cathedrals. I don't look above the sky to seek heaven; my heaven is here on Earth.

~ Satish Kumar

NATURE

When I slow down and tune into my subtle senses,
I find a whole new level of being where plants talk
and stones offer companionship.
The world around me, whether a city lot or a stretch of
protected wilderness, suddenly becomes
alive in a whole new way.
I find teachers and companions that help me learn
what it means to live on the planet Earth.
~ Clea Danaan

In recognizing our power over the tiny lives
we often don't even perceive, Nature grants us an
opportunity to develop respect and
consideration in every footstep.
It also offers an awareness of our individual strength.

~ Eric Alan

NATURE

The pleasure of being so near and in a strange way
intimate with a wild creature of the air
invokes a feeling of privilege.
I feel honoured by such a presence.
~ Sky McCain

Turning onto one side, the whale gazes up at me through the water; looking down into her dark eye, ringed with folds of skin, I meet the lucid and tranquil gaze of an ancestor, one of the ancient ones of the Earth. I feel her taking me out, far out, of thought and linear time, beyond the limited concerns of my ordinary mind, into a profound sense of meeting with another being, whose consciousness is not separate from my own.

~ Eleanor O'Hanlon

NATURE

Indigenous thinking locates human beings as deeply
embedded within and dependent on the land,
a relationship which requires a constant dialogue between
humans and the plants, the animals, and the spirits of
the winds and stars. This viewpoint takes as its starting
position a deep knowing that the world is alive;
I am part of it, and it is part of me.

~ Donna Ladkin

As we all know, there is absolutely no doubt whatsoever
that our species *Homo sapiens* is a member of
the Kingdom called *Animalia*.
In other words, we are animals.
Like all other members of that Kingdom,
we have a slot into which we fit.
~ Marian Van Eyk McCain

NATURE

Deep within the majority of children and adults there is a natural sense of awe and wonder experienced when they look up at the multitude of stars that can be seen at night or contemplate the rich beauty of Earth and its colossal array of plants, flowers, trees, insects, animals and birds.

~ Santoshan (Stephen Wollaston)

Winter can be a good time for us too.
Less pressured to 'do', more time to 'be'.
Time to learn, read, self-educate and prepare for
the season ahead, and perhaps above all,
a time to dream in the darkness.

~ Trevor Sharman

Interconnectedness

5

INTERCONNECTEDNESS

Life has brought us forth. Life is sustaining us.
Life in the form of bees who pollinate,
trees who oxygenate, the oceanic phytoplankton
who help to control the world's climate,
each being playing their part in this interconnected
and interdependent web.

~ Niamh Brennan

[I]f *all* is a part of us and we are a part of the *all*, it then follows that every creature and species is a member of our universal family.

~ Santoshan (Stephen Wollaston)

INTERCONNECTEDNESS

Nature is in us and everywhere and in everything. Even in the heart of the city, Nature is not just the pigeons and rats and cockroaches and mice and the slivers of living green that grow up in the cracks between the paving stones, but all-pervasive.

~ Marian Van Eyk McCain

Spirituality is not about being 'above' the mere physical human reality of our lives; rather it is about embracing it, including and 'being with' all of our experience in a process of integration towards becoming whole.

~ Tania Dolley

INTERCONNECTEDNESS

Nobody can exist alone, we are each of us joined to and simultaneously part of the web that is life, entangled and intertwined with all the other creatures…

~ Niamh Brennan

As I acknowledge the web of connection,
and open myself to what it is saying,
my boundaries become porous to the world around me.
I begin to connect at a bodily,
material level with the world.
I know myself as both an individual
with the capacity for creative action,
and also an integral part of a greater whole.

~ Chris Clarke

INTERCONNECTEDNESS

As I expand my awareness to take in more and more extensive circles of connection, or as I become absorbed in the mystery of intricacy wrapped in the veins and cells of a living leaf, I am sometimes aware of an infinite sustaining power that knits me into this dynamic whole.

~ Chris Clarke

At every level our health is inextricably linked to our connection with the planet. Everything, physical, emotional and spiritual within ourselves resonates with qualities already within creation.

~ June Raymond

INTERCONNECTEDNESS

Our sense of separateness was only ever
a temporary illusion.
Just as every wave is simply part of the ocean,
we are each part of a greater whole.
For Gaia is us and we are Gaia and there is no death,
only constant change and transformation.

~ Marian Van Eyk McCain

There are fires of creativity everywhere

and it's not that we have to somehow learn to be creative;

everything that *is*, is creative.

~ Brian Swimme

Evolvement

6

EVOLVEMENT

We have co-evolved with other life-forms.

Our bodies are made from the same substances.

Our minds have been shaped by interaction with them

since the very beginnings of humanity.

We are inextricably related.

It is not 'us' and 'them'

it is a huge, universal 'we.'

~ Marian Van Eyk McCain

The universe, surely, is more than burning matter.
It has brought forth consciousness in a myriad forms,
of which the human is simply one.
Like the mythical Narcissus gazing obsessively
at his image, captured in one small pool,
we humans became so entranced by our own reflection,
we forgot the depth and magnificence of the life we share
with countless other beings.

~ Eleanor O'Hanlon

EVOLVEMENT

Spiritual and religious traditions' teachings about transformation frequently draw upon the symbolism of death and dying to one's previous self, which is invariably seen as a necessary stage of change and growth to go through in order to awaken to new ways of being.

~ Santoshan (Stephen Wollaston)

The water in your body contains primordial hydrogen
that was created 13.8 billion years ago.
The iron in your blood was created in stars
that are at least 5 billion years old.
All of time, all of evolution is carved into your body.

~ Niamh Brennan

EVOLVEMENT

I understood how each atom, each molecule from the very beginning was imbued with that quality which for lack of a better word could be called love.
That the Great Epic of Evolution of the Universe did not only have a material form but also a spiritual dimension … that from the very beginning, the overriding longing to attract, to bond, to be in relationship, to search for harmony, to love and be loved, had been hardwired into the Universe project:
refined by the evolutionary arrow of time.

~ Erna Colebrook

The true 'frontier' of our evolutionary progress is learning to regard Nature in terms of co-operation and balance. We are just beginning to become conscious of the idea that co-operation in Nature, and in society, is as vital as competition.

~ Nigel Lees

EVOLVEMENT

It's really simple.

Here's the whole story in one line.

This is the greatest discovery of the scientific enterprise:

You take hydrogen gas, and you leave it alone

and it turns into rosebushes, giraffes, and humans.

~ Brian Swimme

Spirituality can be considered a conscious or unconscious belief that relates the individual to the world, and gives meaning and definition to existence.

~ William Fulford

Stories

7

STORIES

Sometimes, it can be a great help to hear from kindred spirits about their ideas and stories. Through this, I know that I am not alone on my quest; others have trodden a similar path and my suffering becomes less detached.

I feel I am part of the flow of the spiritual river and I feel connected once again.

~ Ian Mowll

Eden, I think, is not simply a mythical place,

or a metaphor for original innocence,

or an outworn and divisive religious symbol.

Eden is a state of being,

and we are free to return every time we know ourselves

again in deep communion with the rest of life.

~ Eleanor O'Hanlon

STORIES

We do not all need to be scientists,
nor do we need to be cosmologists,
but we do need to know our own human cosmic story.
Only when we know that story
do we begin to understand our place within it.

~ Grace Blindell

Every creature has a story to tell,
a journey they have made, a wisdom to share;
every creature is, in the words of Meister Eckhart,
'a book about God.' And as we watch and bear witness to
these creatures, perhaps we can learn once again how to be
part of Nature, how to relate to
the other species we share the planet with.

~ Niamh Brennan

STORIES

From that first primordial flaring forth
until this present moment,
every star that has been born and died,
every whirling galaxy and every atom,
every life form that has come and gone,
every earthworm and every cabbage,
all the great forests that have covered the planet,
each unique sunrise and sunset, dance and rhythm,
music, art and poetry, all human emotions,
all human spirituality, the questioning human mind,
the rise of consciousness ~ all, without exception,
are an inseparable part of the ongoing story.

~ Grace Blindell

The story of the Universe is the epic unfolding
of the world, an evolutionary tale of awesome scope.
It speaks of unity and diversity,
of desire and curiosity, of wonder and awe.
It speaks of creativity and imagination,
of death, destruction and transformation.
It is the story of science. It is the story of spirit.
It is the story of all beings, extinct, present and yet to be born.
It is a sacred story of magical unfolding, a story that is
still being born and told in you and me, now.
It is a story, once known, that has the power to inspire our
species into becoming the species we were born to be.

~ Niamh Brennan

STORIES

We are all, in a particular form,

a result of that initial flaring forth,

sharing that same energy, that same divine spark of life.

We share, and are part of, one physical body.

We all breathe the same air, drink the same water,

walk on the same Earth.

We enter the world through the body of another being,

share the same genes and DNA with others;

share the same molecules and atoms which when we die

are released back into the biosphere again to be recycled

into other beings.

~ Niamh Brennan

Studies suggest that explaining the facts of global warming does not change behaviour.
Even though global warming is now irrefutably acknowledged by scientists and that it is 'very likely' that global warming is human induced there has been no wholesale change to our lifestyle
to mitigate climate change.

So, how can change be effected? How can people be motivated to reduce their carbon emissions to make future flooding and climate change less likely?
One way is to tell personal stories. Stories from people that we can understand, relate to, and learn from.

~ Ian Mowll

The Numinous

8

THE NUMINOUS

I know in my heart, beyond all doubt, that a Spirit,
a Consciousness, a creative Being dreamed the cosmos
into existence for ineffable reasons of its own.
I know I am an indissoluble part of this Whole.
I know that, whether we wish to or not, we are still
co-creating our world with each other and Spirit.
And I know that our purpose and responsibility is
to guide the evolution of humanity into the ways
of love and wisdom, beauty and truth.

~ Malcolm Hollick

We have access to the Divine every time we draw a breath, every time we smell a flower, every time we chose to notice the depth of beauty that penetrates the world, fragile and mysterious, gently beseeching us to see and teasing us with its fleeting and intoxicating presence.

~ Niamh Brennan

As we recover a sense of the wild within, we may also come into a new relationship with Nature outside us. Each being in the natural world is beautiful and of value in itself; each is a unique face of the inexpressible, Only Being, the divine Beloved.

~ Neil Douglas-Klotz

Every being has its own interior,

its self, its mystery,

its numinous aspect.

~ Thomas Berry

THE NUMINOUS

There is, from its origin, a pervasive, numinous, guiding mystery in the universe that is designated by different names in different traditions.

~ Thomas Berry

[By] delighting in the Nature that sustains us ... we come to realise that there is something deeper occurring than just living on a planet, some sacred unfolding that is being born right before our eyes, right here, immediate and revealing itself to us, if we only have time to notice...

~ Niamh Brennan

Engagement

9

ENGAGEMENT

It is no longer a case of thinking in terms of whether we and religious and spiritual communities should be getting *jointly* involved in becoming architects of a largely forgotten Earth centred spirituality or not, but about realising that humankind won't be effective enough in bringing about necessary changes if we don't.

~ Santoshan (Stephen Wollaston)

Respect for life extends to other humans too, of course. A billion people worldwide do not have enough to eat, yet the amount of grain fed to cattle to provide the rich west with burgers could alleviate all hunger in the world. The plant food needed to produce just one pound of meat could feed ten people for an entire day.

~ Piers Warren

ENGAGEMENT

One of the aims of green education is to persuade people that reducing consumption is in their own long-term interests as well as those of the planet. Many greens would include amongst those long-term interests a spiritual dimension, for green thought challenges the division between social and spiritual realms.

~ Aidan Rankin

First, it is important to affirm that
every action makes a difference.
In a religious or spiritual perspective such as animism,
where we are all inherently connected within
the fabric of Nature, the smallest action is significant.
Perceiving every part of Nature as animate, soul-full,
shimmering with its own story,
changes how we behave with everything.

~ Emma Restall Orr

ENGAGEMENT

Dream big, then go out and make it happen.

Not just because it's fun and it's the right thing to do.

We have to. There's no waiting around

for technology to save us.

In fact, all the technology we need is right here, right now.

Not just pipes, and systems, and theories.

But spirit, and magic, and most of all, hope.

~ Jonathan Furst

Green spirituality in action can allow the universe itself
to flow through us into the creation of new forms.
Through an ongoing process of relationship ... we can play
a positive part in design, creation and evolution,
help to sustain the diversity of life that makes Gaia thrive;
and hopefully bequeath our role in all this
to our great-great-grandchildren.

~ Jean Boulton

I would propose that sustainability is
a twenty first century word for justice.
Because justice is all about balance,
justice is all about harmony.
Justice is about finding the equilibrium within society,
within human societies connecting to other societies,
to other species and within one's own self
and one's own local relationships.
So justice cuts through all relationships.

~ Matthew Fox

As we recognize the pain of the Earth and
her creatures as our pain, and their beauty as our beauty,
compassion floods our being.
This, combined with skilful actions,
affords the means for restoring wellness to our world.
~ John Travis and Meryn Callander

ENGAGEMENT

We, too, are an intrinsic part of Nature. Our animal bodies, just like the bodies of all other living organisms, are totally made of wild ingredients. Remembering that ~ and living our lives out of that knowledge ~ is the essence of deep green living.

~ Marian Van Eyk McCain

The awareness of our total dependence upon our planet

and our interconnectedness,

will transform us from detached observers

to participants.

~ Grace Blindell

ENGAGEMENT

Authentic spiritual work is only truly effective when it walks hand-in-hand with exterior compassionate work.

~ Santoshan (Stephen Wollaston)

Our responsibility to the Earth is not simply to preserve it,

it is to be present to the earth in its

next sequence of transformations.

~ Thomas Berry

References

REFERENCES

AECC: *Awakening to Earth-Centred Consciousness: Selection from GreenSpirit Magazine.* Edited by Ian Mowll and Santoshan (Stephen Wollaston), Independent Publishing Platform (GreenSpirit Book Series paperback), 2018.

AOR: *All Our Relations: GreenSpirit Connections with the More-than-Human World.* Edited by Marian Van Eyk McCain, GreenSpirit (Book Series paperback), 2016.

DGL: *Deep Green Living.* Edited by Marian Van Eyk McCain, Independent Publishing Platform, (GreenSpirit Book Series paperback), 2016.

DNGS: *Dark Nights of the Green Soul: From Darkness to New Horizons.* Edited by Ian Mowll and Santoshan (Stephen Wollaston), Independent Publishing Platform (GreenSpirit Book Series paperback), 2017.

GS: *GreenSpirit: Path to a New Consciousness.* Edited by Marian Van Eyk McCain, Earth Books, 2010.

MTB: *Meditations with Thomas Berry: With Additional Material by Brian Swimme.* Selected by June Raymond, GreenSpirit, 2010.

PGW: *Pathways of Green Wisdom: Discovering Earth Centred Teachings in Spiritual and Religious Traditions.* Edited by Santoshan (Stephen Wollaston), GreenSpirit (Book Series paperback), 2016.

RGW: *Rivers of Green Wisdom: Exploring Christian and Yogic Earth Centred Spirituality.* By Santoshan (Stephen Wollaston), GreenSpirit (Book Series paperback), 2016.

RWP: *The Rising Water Project: Real Stories of Flooding, Real Stories of Downshifting.* Compiled by Ian Mowll, GreenSpirit (Book Series paperback), 2016.

USSM: *The Universe Story in Science and Myth.* By Greg Morter and Niamh Brennan, GreenSpirit (Book Series paperback), 2016.

WGS: *What is Green Spirituality?* Edited by Marian Van Eyk McCain, GreenSpirit (Book Series paperback), 2016.

Chapter 1: Awakening
p13   GS p152
p14   DNGS p90
p15   WGS p80
p16   DGL p70
p17   RGW p71
p18   GS p184
p19   PGW p36
p20   RGW p70

Chapter 2: GreenSpirit
p23   GS p9
p24   PGW p16
p25   DNGS p107
p26   GS p7
p27   MTB p92
p28   RWP p68
p29   WGS p34
p30   WGS p90

Chapter 3: Earth
p33   GS p189
p34   GS p40
p35   GS p61
p36   WGS p90
p37   GS p236
p38   USSM p29-30

Chapter 4: Nature
p41   AECC p137
p42   GS p3
p43   DGL p103
p44   GS p1
p45   AOR p61
p46   DGL p109
p47   AOR p36
p48   AOR p23
p49   PGW p60
p50   AOR p7
p51   RGW p67
p52   DNGS p24

REFERENCES

Chapter 5: Interconnectedness
- p55 USSM p55-56
- p56 RGW p69
- p57 AOR p8
- p58 GS p82
- p59 GS p75
- p60 AECC p131
- p61 PGW p107
- p62 DNGS p107
- p63 DGL p153
- p64 GS p54

Chapter 6: Evolvement
- p67 AOR p55
- p68 DGL p145-146
- p69 DNGS p13
- p70 USSM p65-66
- p71 AECC p19
- p72 DGL p126
- p73 GS p13
- p74 DNGS p28

Chapter 7: Stories
- p77 DNGS p8
- p78 AOR p23-24
- p79 GS p16
- p80 WGS p23
- p81 GS p19
- p82 USSM p8-9
- p83 USSM p54
- p84 RWP p11

Chapter 8: The Numinous
- p87 WGS p58
- p88 USSM p66
- p89 GS p162
- p90 MTB p41
- p91 MTB p39
- p92 WGS p66-67

Chapter 9: Engagement
- p95   PGW p14
- p96   AECC p103
- p97   PGW p95
- p98   PGW p37-38
- p99   AECC p34
- p100   GS p230
- p101   GS p133
- p102   GS p182
- p103   DGL p100
- p104   GS p123
- p105   RGW p49
- p106   MTB p102

GreenSpirit
Resources

GreenSpirit Book Series & Other Resources

We hope you have enjoyed reading this book, and that it has whetted your appetite to read more in this series and discover the many and varied ways in which green spirituality can be expressed in every single aspect of our lives and culture.

You may also wish to visit our website, which has a members area, information about GreenSpirit's annual events, book reviews and much more: **www.greenspirit.org.uk**

* * *

Other titles in the GreenSpirit Book Series

What is Green Spirituality? Edited by Marian Van Eyk McCain

All Our Relations: GreenSpirit Connections with the More-than-Human World. Edited by Marian Van Eyk McCain

The Universe Story in Science and Myth. By Greg Morter and Niamh Brennan

Rivers of Green Wisdom: Exploring Christian and Yogic Earth Centred Spirituality. By Santoshan (Stephen Wollaston)

Pathways of Green Wisdom: Discovering Earth Centred Teachings in Spiritual and Religious Traditions. Edited by Santoshan (Stephen Wollaston)

Deep Green Living. Edited by Marian Van Eyk McCain

The Rising Water Project: Real Stories of Flooding, Real Stories of Downshifting. Compiled by Ian Mowll

Dark Nights of the Green Soul: From Darkness to New Horizons. Edited by Ian Mowll and Santoshan (Stephen Wollaston)

Awakening to Earth-Centred Consciousness: Selection from GreenSpirit magazine. Edited by Ian Mowll and Santoshan (Stephen Wollaston)

More details on GreenSpirit's website

Free for members ebook editions

GreenSpirit
magazine

GreenSpirit magazine is free for members and is published in both print and electronic form. Each issue includes essential topics connected with Earth-based spirituality. It honours Nature as a great teacher, celebrates the creativity and interrelatedness of all life and of the cosmos, affirms biodiversity and human differences, and honours the prophetic voice of artists.

Find out more at www.greenspirit.org.uk

"For many of us, it's the spirit running through that limitless span of green organisations and ideas that anchors all the work we do. And 'GreenSpirit' is an invaluable source of insight, information and inspiration."
– JONATHON PORRITT.

GreenSpirit
Path to a New Consciousness
Edited by Marian Van Eyk McCain

Only by bringing our thinking back into balance with feeling, intuition and awareness and by grounding ourselves in a sense of the sacred in all things can we achieve a new level of consciousness.

Green spirituality is the key to a new, twenty-first century consciousness. And here is the most comprehensive book ever written on green spirituality.

Published by Earth Books
ISBN 978-1-84694-290-7
282 pages

Meditations with Thomas Berry
With additional material by Brian Swimme
Selected by June Raymond

Selected and arranged by June Raymond, especially for GreenSpirit Books, this is a collection of profound and inspiring quotations from one of the most important voices of our times, the late Thomas Berry, author, geologian, cultural historian and lover of the Earth.

Published by GreenSpirit
ISBN 978-0-9552157-4-2
111 pages

Printed in Great Britain
by Amazon